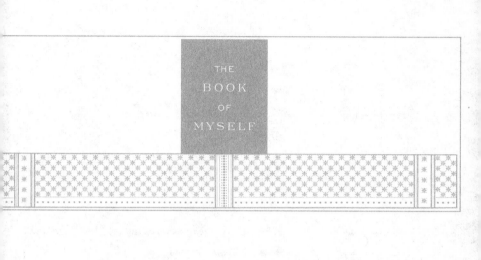

THE
BOOK
OF
MYSELF

THE
LIFE STORY
OF

....
(Name)

....
(Dates)

The Book of Myself

A DO-IT-YOURSELF AUTOBIOGRAPHY
IN 201 QUESTIONS

CARL & DAVID MARSHALL

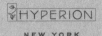

HYPERION

NEW YORK

Hyperion books are available for special promotions and premiums.
For details contact the HarperCollins Special Markets Department
in the New York office at 212-207-7528, fax 212-207-7222,
or email spsales@harpercollins.com.

Design by Shubhani Sarkar

10 9 8 7 6

TO OUR CHILDREN

GENE AND KARLDENE, EMILY AND BENJAMIN

....

As your teachers we have become humble students

CONTENTS

HOW?

- Here are 201 prompts to help you begin telling your special story. You fill in the rest.

- Three main sections, or chronological life phases, cover the early, middle, and later years. It is up to you to decide where one section leaves off and the next begins for your own life.

- Each phase of life is broken down into five subjects, covering experiences about family, friends, education, work, and the world. These subjects are located at the top of the page.

- The table of contents will help you find a particular life phase and subject quickly, so start anywhere you want.

WHO AND WHEN?

- If you are ninety-one years old, like one of the coauthors, you are in a position to write down almost the whole story. Get help from your loved ones to remember special moments.

- If you are one or two generations younger, you can still start the story, since at least your early years are now behind you and the memories are still fresh in your mind. Or if there is a family member or friend whose life you are interested in, ask him or her to fill out this book for you, or use it to interview the person and record his or her answers.

- If you are still in your early years, you can start the story and fill it out as you go. By searching ahead for experiences yet to come, you may recognize them as they appear. Or give the book to a loved one to fill out and return to you.

- If you are studying your family's genealogy, fill out as much as you can for each person you are researching. It might take some digging, but the result will add color to the leaves of the family tree you are developing.

WHAT DO I DO WITH THIS BOOK AFTER IT IS FILLED OUT?

- Give it to your children, grandchildren, or a special friend. They will treasure your written story as a connection to you and to the family history.

- This might just be the beginning. You may be left inspired to add additional stories in a separate notebook, scrapbook, or on pages to tuck into this journal.

- This journal is complete when you say it is. You do not have to fill out all the questions. Fill in only what you want.

- Keep it with your family heirlooms, for your own pleasure and for future generations.

- If you are using this to write about someone else's life, celebrate the person's life by sharing your discoveries and gems with other family members.

- Most of all, enjoy the stories. Read it from cover to cover; reflect and rejoice in the wonder of life's experiences.

I WAS BORN in 1903 and have just celebrated my ninety-first birthday with Gladys, my wife of sixty-eight years. We have a son and daughter, eight wonderful grandchildren, and so many great-grandchildren that I cannot keep track of them all. Two years ago, my daughter, Karldene, helped me write my memoirs. It was an exhilarating experience to tell the stories of my childhood, young adulthood, and later years in a way that could be passed on to future generations. My family loved it. My friends were envious, but most of them felt it would be too difficult for them to do the same. After all, it took me over a year to write it, with my daughter doing all the typing and assembling.

So when my grandson David approached me with a plan for a simple book that would help people begin telling their stories, I jumped at the chance to co-write it. What we have done here is give you the skeleton for your story. You'll provide the meat that goes on the bones. After all, everyone has stories to tell about family, friends, education, work, and the world during the different phases of life.

I am nearing the end of my journey now. But before I go, I wanted my family and loved ones to know my stories, big or small, deep or shallow, known or unknown. I have learned a lot during these last nine decades and want to share this with the next three generations. I know you do, too, before you go. Let them know.

CARL E. MARSHALL

(Grandpa Carl passed away prior to the publication of this book.)

I grew up in the 1960s and 1970s and just celebrated my fiftieth birthday with Kate, my wife of over twenty years. We have two children, one off to college and another leaving the nest next year. Our grandparents have now all passed away, and we are watching our own parents grow older with trepidation and awe; trepidation in realizing that they will not be with us forever, and awe in realizing the wisdom about life they carry with them. Grandpa Carl taught me to reach for the stars and to believe in myself even if others lose their faith. He also worked me hard—but I have to admit, such tasks as bricklaying in his backyard helped strengthen my work ethic. And he showed me how to treat math as an adventure instead of a chore.

I have always loved hearing Grandpa spin yarns around the dinner table. They helped me to know him more intimately. I wanted to find a way to ask him about all the different areas of his life and to save what he told me, even some of the little tidbits that he would never think to add himself. It now comforts me to know that long after Grandpa Carl is gone, I will still have this little book of treasures to share with my children and grandchildren. I hope this collection of life stories will help you to begin sharing your stories with those who will follow in your path.

DAVID P. MARSHALL

EARLY
YEARS

THIS is how people described me as a child, and how I saw myself:

SOME of my favorite games, toys, or ways to entertain myself were:

....

....

....

....

....

....

....

....

....

....

....

....

....

....

....

....

....

....

....

WE had these pets or access to these other animals growing up:

I would describe each of my brothers, sisters, or cousins when we
were young this way:

SOME of my mother's traits that I admired or appreciated were:

IF I had any trouble with my mother growing up, it was in this area:

SOME of my father's traits that I admired or appreciated were:

IF I had any trouble with my father while I was young, it was in this area:

....

....

....

....

....

....

....

....

....

....

....

....

....

....

....

....

....

....

....

MY parents felt strongly about passing on these lessons:

....

....

....

....

....

....

....

....

....

....

....

....

....

....

....

....

....

....

....

....

....

....

THIS gift really sticks in my memory:

MY godparent or a special adult in my life growing up was:

I remember our house, neighborhood, and family car this way:

A habit, characteristic, or value I picked up during my early years
was:

OUR family usually ate breakfast, lunch, and dinner in these ways:

THIS is what we usually did at Thanksgiving or another major holiday:

OUR family celebrated Christmas, Hanukkah, or other religious
holidays in these ways:

THIS person in my family stood out from the rest (as funnier, more
   studious, messier, more temperamental . . .):

....

....

....

....

....

....

....

....

....

....

....

....

....

....

....

....

....

....

....

....

I really got into trouble (or should have) when I did this:

HERE are a few of today's modern conveniences we didn't have, and how we managed:

MY family's first TV or computer was in the year _____. My
favorite TV or software programs were:

....

....

....

....

....

....

....

....

....

....

....

....

....

....

....

....

....

....

THIS was a favorite time with my siblings or other family members:

THIS significant illness or injury scared me:

I remember these things about my grandmother(s):

AND I remember these things about my grandfather(s):

IF I remember anything about my great-grandparents, it is this:

MY ancestors came from these parts of the world:

MY best friend during childhood was:

THIS person appealed to me because of certain characteristics (talent, smarts, good looks, athletic skill . . .) or common interests:

I was generally popular, unpopular, or somewhere in between
   because:

I wanted to be friends with this person or type of person, but
   couldn't:

THIS was a memorable birthday party or celebration with my friends:

....

....

....

....

....

....

....

....

....

....

....

....

....

....

....

....

....

....

....

....

....

I had a childhood crush on this person:

MY first young sweetheart was:

I am proud to have helped this friend by:

WHAT my friends and I liked best to do together was:

THIS was a particularly dangerous or scary thing I did with my friends:

IF my parents had only known! I did this forbidden thing with my
    friends:

THIS person significantly influenced my life during these years:

ONE of my earliest memories about school was:

....

....

....

....

....

....

....

....

....

....

....

....

....

....

....

....

....

....

....

....

....

I really enjoyed or hated this grade in elementary school:

ONE of my most memorable teachers in elementary school was:

I remember these nonclassroom activities (recess, lunchtime, field
trips . . .):

WHEN I was a young child, I fantasized about having this job when
I grew up:

....
....
....
....
....
....
....
....
....
....
....
....
....
....
....
....
....
....
....
....
....
....

I liked this subject a lot in junior high or high school:

I had some trouble with this subject in junior high or high school:

ONE of my most memorable teachers in junior high or high school
was:

I really enjoyed or hated this grade in junior high or high school:

THIS is how I got to school each morning in my early years:

THESE were my favorite sports to watch or play:

WHAT I enjoyed doing most after school was:

....
....
....
....
....
....
....
....
....
....
....
....
....
....
....
....
....
....
....

A particular assignment or type of homework I enjoyed was (science
project, book report, spelling lists . . .):

I would describe my K–12 schools as (size, kind of students,
strengths, reputation . . .):

MY teachers generally described me as this kind of student:

I remember my high school graduation or similar rite of passage:

IF I attended college or trade school, this is where I went and how I picked it:

....

....

....

....

....

....

....

....

....

....

....

....

....

....

....

....

....

....

....

....

ONE of my strongest memories from college or trade school is:

....
....
....
....
....
....
....
....
....
....
....
....
....
....
....
....
....
....
....

MY favorite mentor or role model in college or trade school was:

THIS is one of the most important things about life I learned during
my years in school:

MY religious training growing up was:

I remember these chores during my early years:

MY first job for pay was:

I enjoyed this particular work assignment:

I took care of this person or animal growing up:

I hated this responsibility or job, but it has served me well as an
   adult:

THINGS I remember about my mother's work and responsibilities were:

I remember these things about my father's work and responsibilities:

OTHER family members had these jobs or duties when I was young:

....

....

....

....

....

....

....

....

....

....

....

....

....

....

....

....

....

....

....

....

THIS is the profession that I often considered as a teenager and how
   I learned about it:

....

....

....

....

....

....

....

....

....

....

....

....

....

....

....

....

....

....

....

....

I liked this kind of music and these musicians growing up:

THE "in" things of my youth were (clothing styles, colors, hairstyles, lingo, other fads . . .):

THESE were some of my favorite actors or celebrities and what I
   liked about them:

IN my early years, the parts of the world I knew best and that
interested me the most were:

THIS major event marked a turning point in the world when I was
   young (D-Day, fall of Saigon or the Berlin Wall, the Gulf War . . .):

MY memories of the biggest war or serious conflict that occurred
   during my early years are these:

....

....

....

....

....

....

....

....

....

....

....

....

....

....

....

....

....

....

....

I remember when these discoveries or technological advances were made:

THIS was another big news story I remember from when I was
young:

MY parents and other family members felt this way about politics:

MIDDLE
YEARS

THESE are some interesting things about my siblings or cousins in
our middle years:

....

....

....

....

....

....

....

....

....

....

....

....

....

....

....

....

....

....

....

....

AUNTS, uncles, and other relatives who kept close after I left home
were:

....

....

....

....

....

....

....

....

....

....

....

....

....

....

....

....

....

....

....

....

I regret losing touch with these family members over the years:

MY parents supported me in these ways:

AS an adult, I saw these notable characteristics in my mother:

. . . .

. . . .

. . . .

. . . .

. . . .

. . . .

. . . .

. . . .

. . . .

. . . .

. . . .

. . . .

. . . .

. . . .

. . . .

. . . .

. . . .

. . . .

. . . .

AS an adult, I noticed these prominent characteristics in my father:

THIS issue caused a rift between my parents and me, and this is
how it turned out:

....

....

....

....

....

....

....

....

....

....

....

....

....

....

....

....

....

....

....

....

THESE were some of my experiences and relationships while
  looking for love:

MY first serious romance was with:

THIS is how I met my sweetheart, fell in love, and became engaged:

A few highlights from our wedding and honeymoon were:

THIS is how we decided whether to have children and how many:

I remember the births of our children (or other young relatives):

I recall these funny incidents about our children (or other young relatives):

THESE pets or other animals were part of my daily life:

IF I never married, or if I got divorced, this is why:

THIS was a particularly memorable vacation, reunion, or gathering:

SOME of the things I loved doing with my family were:

MY parents played this kind of grandparent role:

THIS health problem or accident was very scary for my family:

THIS was a difficulty we faced as a family and here's how we
handled it:

A lonely or hard time for me or one of my family members was:

WHEN the children left the nest, this is where they went and what they did:

I was a good parent (uncle, aunt, mentor . . .) in these ways:

IN this area, I think I could have been a better parent (aunt, uncle, mentor . . .):

MY best friend after I left home was:

THESE people were very dear friends to me in my middle
  years:

....

....

....

....

....

....

....

....

....

....

....

....

....

....

....

....

....

....

....

....

....

THIS is a sport I enjoyed playing, watching, or attending with friends:

ONE of the ways I liked to entertain friends and guests was:

MY friends and I had fun doing this activity together:

I remember this funny or embarrassing incident with a good friend:

THIS is how my friends and I helped each other through difficult times:

WHEN I think of compassion and goodness I think of this person:

ONE big misunderstanding I had with a friend was:

I was very hurt by this person I counted as a friend:

I learned to open up and take myself less seriously through my
friendship with this person:

OVER the years, I learned that true friendship means:

....

....

....

....

....

....

....

....

....

....

....

....

....

....

....

....

....

....

....

....

....

....

THIS book, lecture, movie, article, or show had a very strong
impact on me:

I enjoyed these kinds of books, magazines, newspapers, and TV
programs during my middle years:

AFTER my formal education period, this is how I continued my lifelong learning:

....

....

....

....

....

....

....

....

....

....

....

....

....

....

....

....

....

....

....

....

THESE are some new skills I learned in my middle years (and how
I learned them):

I was able to learn these things quickly and easily:

LEARNING this new skill as an adult was quite a challenge
(bridge, skiing, golf, computer . . .):

EVEN as an adult, I thought of this person as my "teacher," and this
is what I learned:

THIS was something I was able to teach well to others:

HERE is where I found spiritual guidance and education as an adult:

THIS is something I learned the hard way:

ONE area I wish I had been able to learn more about or further
explore as an adult was:

SOME of my home and family responsibilities were:

MY profession and the companies or institutions I worked for were:

THINGS I liked and disliked about my work included:

ONE of my favorite co-workers, bosses, or work-related people was:

....

....

....

....

....

....

....

....

....

....

....

....

....

....

....

....

....

....

....

....

....

THIS person was a role model or mentor who helped me in my
career:

ONE of the most difficult people (boss, coworker, client) I worked
  with was:

....

....

....

....

....

....

....

....

....

....

....

....

....

....

....

....

....

....

....

ONE of the biggest mistakes I made in my work life was:

IF I could have changed professions in midstream I would have become:

I am proud of these career accomplishments:

IF I could have changed the balance between time spent at work,
with family, and at play, I would have:

THIS is how I worked to keep in good health during my middle
    years:

I put a lot of time and effort into this hobby:

MY experience with the military or politics as an adult was:

THIS is how I served my community:

MY advice to young people just starting their work lives is:

THESE are the presidents or politicians who most impressed me:

I remember what I was doing when this tragic event happened (JFK or MLK assassination, Iranian hostage crisis, Chernobyl, 9/11, Hurricane Katrina . . .):

THE clothing fashions and hairstyles I wore during these adult years were:

I made these significant purchases (house, car, boat, plane
tickets . . .) and this is what I paid:

SOME of my favorite movies, TV shows, and stars were:

THIS is what I was doing when this dramatic achievement occurred (first moon walk, polio vaccine invented, home-run record set . . .):

THESE travel experiences made an impression on me, and this is
what they taught me:

....

....

....

....

....

....

....

....

....

....

....

....

....

....

....

....

....

....

....

....

I felt part of the larger world when I personally witnessed or was
involved in this (election, Olympics, political protest, overseas
assignment . . .):

I felt that these things were going right or wrong in the world during
my middle years:

LATER
YEARS

MY family provided nurture and moral support to me in these ways:

I wish I had seen more of this family member during my elder years:

THIS friend became like a member of my family in my later years:

MY siblings and cousins did these things as adults:

I remember when my grandchildren (or other relatives) were born:

I treasure this special time with my grandchildren (or other special young people):

THIS is what I predict for each of my grandchildren (or other special young people):

....

....

....

....

....

....

....

....

....

....

....

....

....

....

....

....

....

....

....

....

....

....

THE strengths and characteristics of each of my children (or other
   adult relatives) are:

....

....

....

....

....

....

....

....

....

....

....

....

....

....

....

....

....

....

....

THE best and hardest parts about marriage are:

I believe that strong and healthy families have these things in common:

IF I could change something in my family life, it would be this:

THESE deaths in the family affected me strongly:

....

....

....

....

....

....

....

....

....

....

....

....

....

....

....

....

....

....

....

....

....

I think I have this characteristic or tendency more now than in my
earlier years:

OF all my personality traits, I hope my family will remember this one about me:

WHEN I look back on my life, one of my favorite periods was:

I learned that living a fulfilling life includes these important things:

IN my later years, my attitude toward death and dying has been:

I am glad to have made these new friends in my later years:

THIS friend accomplished something truly remarkable:

THINGS I look for in a friend in my later years are:

WHAT I like to do most with friends is:

A funny thing that happened to me and a friend was:

THESE are some good jokes my friends and I exchanged:

I stayed by these friends as they went through some tough times:

THIS person stuck by me through thick and thin:

I was sad when this dear friend died:

THIS good friend taught me this important lesson about life:

NEVER too old to learn something new, I learned this in my later
   years:

AFTER I retired, I took classes in the following areas:

THESE were some highlights of my favorite or most enlightening travel:

....

....

....

....

....

....

....

....

....

....

....

....

....

....

....

....

....

....

....

SOME games and shows are also educational. This has been one of my favorites:

OF all the cultural arts, I enjoy this one the most:

I learned a lot from getting involved with this cause or group:

MY relationship to formal worship or religion during my later years
has been:

....

....

....

....

....

....

....

....

....

....

....

....

....

....

....

....

....

....

EVEN after I officially "retired," I still did this kind of work:

I retired in this place with these people:

THIS is what I learned over the years about managing money:

THIS is what I have done to keep healthy and in good physical
shape later in life:

THESE conditions have made my medical doctors important to me:

SOME of my favorite meals or recipes have been:

THIS hobby or habit has given me lots of satisfaction in later years:

THIS kind of work or activity kept me young:

IN hindsight, I might have done this differently in my life:

WHEN I look back on my life's work, these are my most prized accomplishments:

THESE were my favorite movies, TV shows, and books during
retirement:

I admire these important people for making a difference in the world:

THIS big event had a strong effect on me during my later years:

MY views about some things have changed over the years (politics, money, parenting, social issues . . .):

SOMETIMES I felt as though I was out of step with the rest of the world on certain issues:

....

....

....

....

....

....

....

....

....

....

....

....

....

....

....

....

....

....

....

....

....

MY hopes for the nation and world are:

....
....
....
....
....
....
....
....
....
....
....
....
....
....
....
....
....
....
....

WHAT the world will remember about my generation is:

IF I could write my own obituary or epitaph, it would say:

CARL E. MARSHALL was raised in rural Oklahoma and received his bachelor's and master's degrees in mathematics from Oklahoma State University, and his doctorate in statistics from Iowa State. He became a professor of mathematics at OSU and created the university's graduate program in statistics. He was known by his colleagues as "Mr. Statistics of Oklahoma."

DAVID P. MARSHALL is the coauthor, with his wife, Kate, of *The Book of Us: A Journal of Your Love Story in 150 Questions*, *The Book of My Pet: In Celebration of Pets* and *What I Love About You*. Other Marshall books include *Words to Live By: A Journal of Wisdom for Someone You Love*, by Emily and Kate Marshall. He lives with his family in northern California.

If you have any thoughts about the book, please send them to:

David P. Marshall
P.O. Box 6846
Moraga, CA 94570–6846

Or email them to *marshallbooks@gmail.com*

And visit *www.marshallbooks.net*